# Alphabet Meditations for Teachers

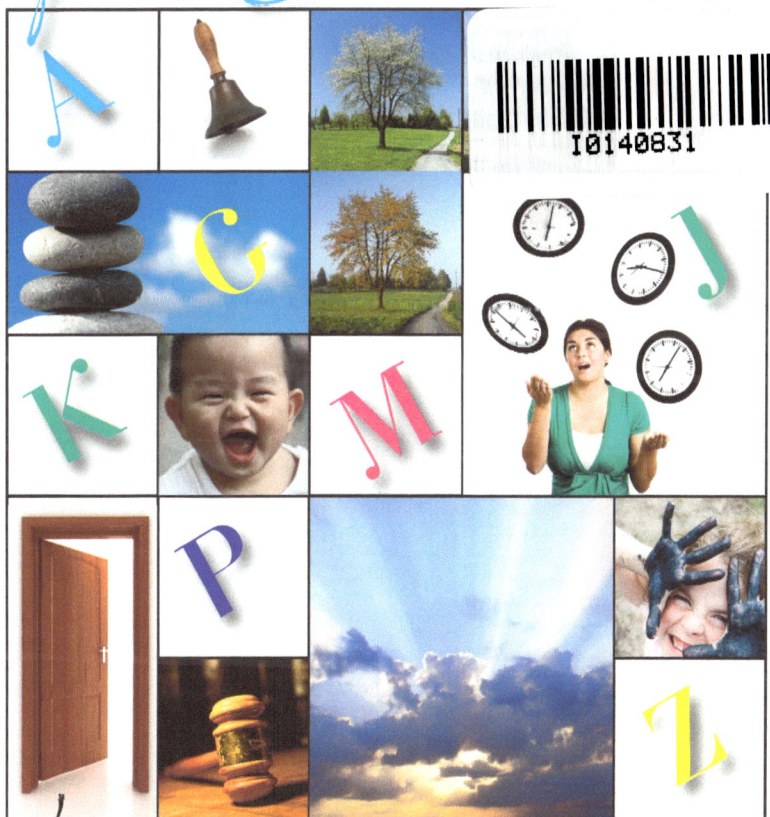

Nancy Oelklaus, Ed.D

Alphabet Meditations for Teachers: Everyday Inspiration for Educators
Copyright © 2009 by Nancy Oelklaus. All Rights Reserved.

First Edition: April 2009

---

Library of Congress Cataloging-in-Publication Data

Oelklaus, Nancy, 1943-
  Alphabet meditations for teachers : everyday inspiration for educators / by Nancy Oelklaus. -- 1st ed.
      p. cm.
  ISBN-13: 978-1-932690-88-0 (trade paper : alk. paper)
  ISBN-10: 1-932690-88-3 (trade paper : alk. paper)
  1. Teaching--Miscellanea. 2. Teachers--Conduct of life. 3. Motivation in education.  I. Title.
  LB1025.3.O37 2009
  371.1--dc22

                              2009004301

Distributed by: Ingram Book Group, New Leaf Distributing, Quality Books.

Published by:
Loving Healing Press          info@LHPress.com
5145 Pontiac Trail            www.LHPress.com
Ann Arbor, MI 48105-9627

Tollfree 888-761-6268
Fax 734-663-6861

Loving Healing Press

## Educators Praise *Alphabet Meditations*

"Although I do not do much reading for pleasure, I could not stop reading *Alphabet Meditations for Teachers*. Its brief, concise, poetic style makes it an easy, relaxing read. The author's love for teachers, children, and the differences that exist among us clearly came through. I absolutely recommend this book as preferred reading for the Master Teacher."

—Doug Rogers, Executive Director
Association of Texas Professional Educators (ATPE)

"*Alphabet Meditations for Teachers* is an inspirational must-read for educators, as well as others who work with children in non-academic settings—social workers, nurses, and child care givers. Actually everyone who interacts with young people will find this book a treasure of wise advice for communicating compassionately with youth."

—Judy Farmer, Executive Director
Texas School Public Relations Association

"*Alphabet Meditations for Teachers* is a thoughtful, inspiring, and well done piece—a perfect gift for teachers. It accurately reflects some of the most haunting thoughts excellent teachers have, overworked, yet caring as they struggle with all the demands of their jobs."

—Sherry Anderson, Adjunct instructor at Central Michigan University, and a retired school administrator.

"*Alphabet Meditations for Teachers* is a most needed antidote to the toxic side effects of our accumulated reactions to institutional rigidity and regimentation. Free of pretentiousness, Nancy Oelklaus' meditations are at once grounded in lucid accounts of teacher experience and courageous devotions to authentic work and love."

—Caroline Eick, Ph.D.
Assistant Professor, Education Department
Mount St. Mary's University, Emmitsburg, MD

"*Alphabet Meditations* provides powerful tools for supporting the important work that teachers do every minute of every day. Many of the poems provide a respite and a space for reflection. They provide another perspective and reveal assumptions we make from our experiences. They help us refresh, reflect, renew, and rethink. We need to arise anew each day for the children!"

—De Ann Currin, PhD
Elliott Elementary School Principal, Lincoln, NE

"*Alphabet Meditations* is poetry that speaks about the essence of teaching. It will touch your heart and soul so that you may better connect to the hearts, minds, and souls of all those you teach. As you read and reflect upon these meditations may they nourish your soul and remind you why you choose to teach."

—Cindy Isaacson
Special Education Teacher, Austin, TX

"Dr. Oelklaus's *Alphabet Meditations for Teachers* is a gentle, but firm, reminder that we need to meet the needs of students for them to learn...and they are not all the same. Her meditations provide insight into building resilience, holding high expectations for all – no excuses, and for attending to the gifts those children bring to the classroom... she pushes teachers toward serving the head and heart needs of all children with excellence, compassion, and responsibility."

—Sandra K Darling, PhD,
Learning Bridges, Chandler, AZ

"*Alphabet Meditations for Teachers* by Nancy Oelklaus tugs at the heart strings of all teachers who yearn for wisdom in seeking the answers to those struggles and frustrations faced by our profession. Read it to learn, read it to grow, read it to remember."

—Sherry Henderson, Principal
Trinity Episcopal School, Marshall, TX

To my mentors,
Pat Smith and Grace Grimes,
women of intelligence, courage, and heart

And to my students
who accepted the gift I had to give.

## About the Author

A native of southwest Oklahoma, Nancy Oelklaus began her career as a high school English teacher in Marshall, Texas. She earned the B.A. in Communications, cum laude, from Oklahoma Baptist University, the M.A. in English from the University of North Texas and the doctorate in educational administration from Texas A&M University, Commerce, where she was named an outstanding graduate.

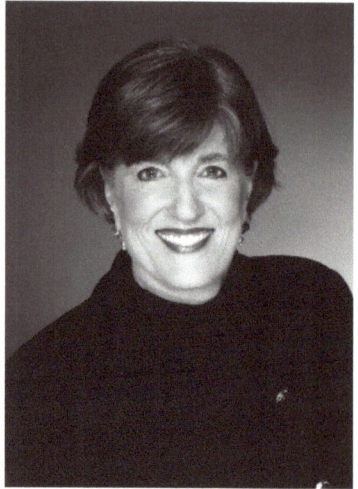

For nine years she served as assistant superintendent for instructional services in Marshall, TX, followed by nine years as executive director for the Texas Association for Supervision and Curriculum Development.

Throughout her career, Nancy has been a speaker and workshop leader throughout the U.S. She has also conducted workshops in Jakarta, Indonesia, Singapore, and The Netherlands. Also, she has designed and facilitated processes for developing school boards.

Her articles have appeared in *The American School Board Journal*, *The Austin Business Journal*, *The Systems Thinker*, and *Austin Woman Magazine*. She is the author of *Journey from Head to Heart: Living and Working Authentically* (Ann Arbor, Michigan: Loving Healing Press, 2008). Three coaching CDs by Nancy are available through Amazon.

# The Invisible School

When people think of school, the image that comes to mind are the buildings, the classes, the activities, the books and lessons. But beyond all of that is the invisible school—the billions of neuronal patterns that each of us is carrying around inside our heads. How we think about school. How we feel about each other while we are at school. The electromagnetic fields that each of us is sending and receiving. This is the invisible school.

When I was a school administrator, I used to marvel that a student who behaved perfectly in one teacher's class would be a "holy terror" for another instructor. Now I understand a wee bit more about the electromagnetic field that each one of us emits. I've learned from observing my own relationships that things go better when I'm thinking and feeling positively toward the other person. I've learned that when I shift the energy in myself through adjusting my thinking, the problem "out there" dissipates.

The challenge is to reframe or tell ourselves a different story about the people around us so that we can work with them well. When this happens, students become more teachable; colleagues become more congenial; school becomes a happier place to be.

I wish I had known this when I was teaching in the classroom. I wish I had known it as an administrator. I didn't. I thought my most important job was to achieve goals and objectives—to teach the curriculum. But now I understand that the curriculum is only one strand of the work. The other is inspiring students to integrate that curriculum into their memory and operational systems. The teacher's role is to integrate head and heart so that students both achieve and become confident human beings who know they are valued. May these meditations inspire you to be a power for good in your school.

# A to Z

Alpha and Omega—
Beginning and End—
Circular, Cyclical
Meaning,

Deafened by
Clocks, Papers, and Bells.

Look me up—
To the circular stars—
The cyclical orbs—
To know I matter.

Look me up—
To the circular/slanted
Eyes that trust me—
To know they matter.

# A is for Adam

His name is Adam;
Her name is Eve.
Surname doesn't matter.
They are All Children.
They are My Children—
Not mine—
Ours.

I am their leader,
Their guide.
Not their master.
They trust me.

They trust me to love
The shape—
Or color—
Of their eyes and hair.

They trust me to see their
Natural beauty, hiding behind
Designer labels—expensive goods
On their feet—or backs.

They trust me not to care
That their clothes come
From charity.

They trust me not to try
To fix them,
But to love them.

To love their tough swagger
Until they let their brains
And hearts relax.

To love them into knowing,
Thinking, creating,
Believing that they can.

They trust me to choose well
What I teach them.
They trust me to sense when
It's not working, and change.

They trust me to know there is
More than one way to learn.

They trust me not to give up on them,
Even though they make it tough,
And it would be so easy
To walk away.

I'm here for a purpose.
They trust me;
I'm worthy of their trust.

Fill me today with
Creative strength of
Creative trust.
Help me trust them,

## B is for Bells

Bells are driving me nuts.

They control my
Every move—decision.
I hear them in my dreams—
Or nightmares.

They stop thought
With their shrill—
Or soft—
Intrusion.

My eyes move from
The eyes of the souls before me
To the clock on the wall,
And I shirk their questions

Or stall, saying,
"We'll continue tomorrow."
But tomorrow, the moment is gone.
I—or they—forget.

The clock is not
My master,
Nor am I its slave,
Unless I will it.

Find for me
Alternatives to
Rigidity—
To Mechanistic Models.

Give me the courage
To ask the question,
What can we do
About bells?

Give me the freedom
Of mind and heart
To find
Solutions.

# C Is for Change

Change is such a
Normal part of my
Daily existence.
Why do I resist it so—
Within?

In the schoolyard, I watch
The differential effects of
Differential elements—
Rain, heat, light.

As seasons march across
My life, I welcome—
Embrace—each one for the
Freshness—rebirth—it brings.

Is any spring the
Same as the last?
Azaleas are brighter or
Dimmer or thinner.

Bluebonnets are more—
Or less—plentiful,
More—or less—
Tall or thick.

In my home I search for
Variety—betterment—
With new or rearranged
Furnishings—appliances.

The children I teach change
Daily. I watch them lose a
Tooth—or survive the First Date.

So why—oh why—am I
So reluctant to change
My lesson plan?
The way I teach?

I understand that
Holding my craft firm
Is unnatural—
Clinging to false security.

It's forcing myself not to
Grow, like Chinese women
Who bound their daughters'
feet.
Help me not do that

To myself—or these
Dear Children I teach.
Help me—today—
To grow.

# D Is for Do

The "don't" messages
Assail us.
We're the pinball,
Trying to get to the highest hole,
Buffeted by barriers
Clanging, DON'T!
When we hit them.

As a pinball,
I would like it better
If someone would
Whisper the DO'S to me
So I don't have to
Discover the DON'TS
So rudely.

Help me ask for the
DO'S when I feel myself
Chafing against the DON'TS
Help me listen
To my students' voices
And hearken to their eyes
As they ask me.

Where are the DO'S?
DO trust the spirit
Within me to
Love me and tell me
The right thing to do.
DO love and value
Who I am.

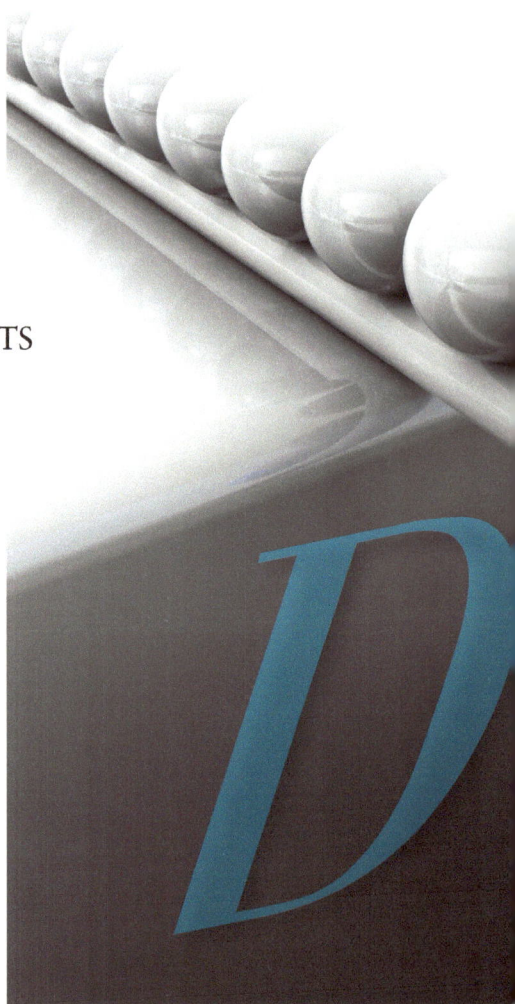

DO accept others
Just as they are.
DO open my mind to learn,
Knowing God is my guide,
To help me sort the
Junk from the valuables.
DO accept that guidance.

Help me live these words
Today—just today.
Help me teach, through a
Living model,
The great ultimate
DO'S of life.
Grant me wisdom to learn them.

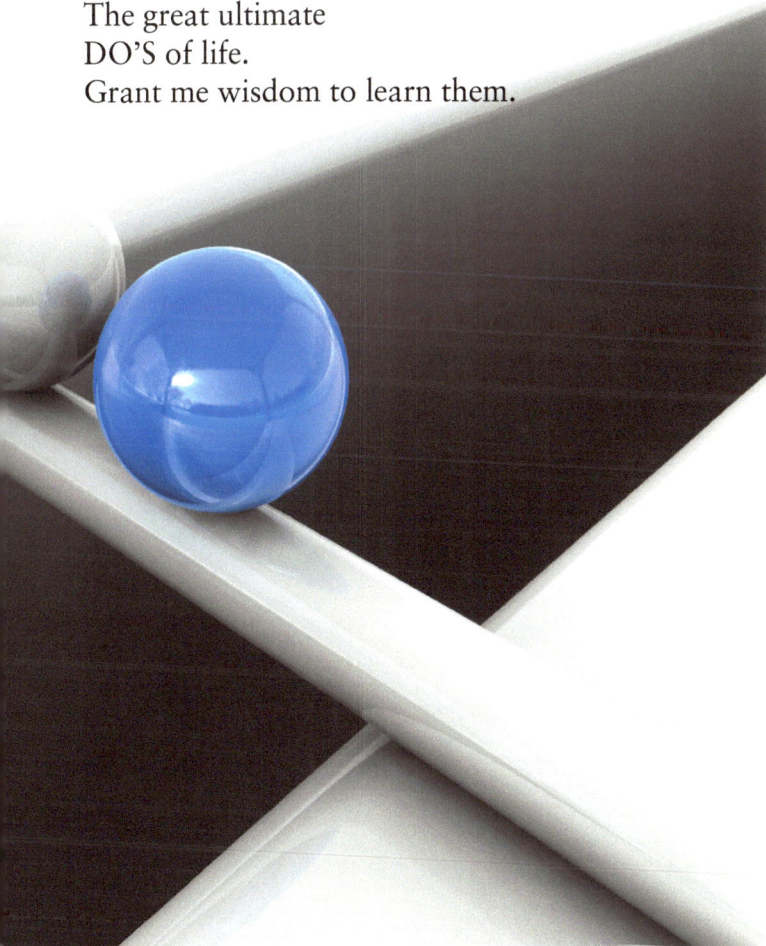

# E Is for Excellence

Excellence is a word
I keep hearing.
When it's spoken,
We all nod and agree.

No one ever asks,
"What is it?"
We pretend to know it
And do it.

But if we're doing it,
Why are people screaming
At us
That we're not?

Help me realize
That the child
Whose look could kill
Is telling me

He doesn't think
My work
Looks like excellent,
So she's checked out—

Mentally—spiritually—
Personally—and completely.
Help me realize
I can't declare excellence

And ignore the
Eyes of the
Sons and daughters
Daily before me.

Help me know
I can't deny
The claim of the world
That we're hiding from them.

Help me ask You,
"What is excellent?"
When you answer,
Help me listen and do.

## F is for Fear

I know, with all my heart,
That a fear-driven
School is not a good place
For people.

Our brains shut down,
Reduced to the most
Elemental—elementary
Learning. We can't think well.

Search my soul
To feel my own fears.
Help me know how to
Release them—just let go.

Write on my heart the
Ancient Lesson that
Perfect Love casts out fear.

Help me feel that
Love. Let it ease
My fear.

Help me remember that
Test scores, evaluations,
Public censure and
Petty spats

Do not define who I
Really am. I am a
Perfect child of Divine Love,
Entrapped by fear.

Unloose
The ropes. Help me
Feel the freedom of
Your love.

Then—only then—
Can I reach out
To my students
In trust and love,

Help them find their fears,
And love them away.

## G Is for Grades

How I hate grades!
I make an imperfect test
For them to "pass,"
Making me
Their judge and executioner.

Then they compare,
Each to each.
Some walk out
With superior air;
Others pretend not to care.

Help me reflect
On what I'm doing—
Or not doing—
With grades.
Am I fair?

If I'm fair,
Am I right?
Right with what I test?
Right with how I average?
Or am I the designer of a game?

Help me answer
This question:
What difference
Does it make?
What am I *really* measuring?

How many times
Does a student who makes F
Need to be told
He's an F
Before his spirit breaks?

Or a C student,
That she's mediocre?
Or A students,
That they're grand?
Or me, that I'm powerful?

Oh, help me know
That in your eyes
We're all precious,
Perfect children of Divine Love.
Help me reflect that love.

## H Is for Happiness

Happiness shouldn't be so
Foreign to a classroom.
Why did I believe the
Old adage,
"Don't smile until Christmas"?

Being mean induces fear.
Fear's not a good
Place to be.
It limits learning.
So why do I play this game?

Because it was
Done to me,
So I repeat
The errors
Of the ages?

Help me
Accept happiness
In my life
And share it
With those I teach—

With those I
Teach alongside—
With those who
Sweep the halls
Or serve the trays.

With those who
Smile at me
And those who don't.

Help me know
Happiness isn't
Trying to make
Everyone else
Happy.

It's a feeling within
Of knowing who I am,
Entering on what I believe,
And simply
Living it—

Sharing it—
Daily.
Help me
Today
To be happy.

# *I* is for Imagination

Imagination is where they are
When their eyes glaze—
Or heads nod—
When they seem not to care.

What are they imagining?
Or is it fantasizing?
Walks in outer space?
Frolics with friends?

Love's first awareness?
Fights they've had?
Family's trouble or triumph?
How do they see themselves?

I can't know—
It's not mine to see.
But I know their
Imagination is real.

Sometimes I say,
"They just aren't creative."
But I know
It's not so.

I just haven't found
The way to guide
What I teach
Into their creative stream.

That's it! There's a
Stream called Imagination.
My job is to find a
Launch for my canoe.

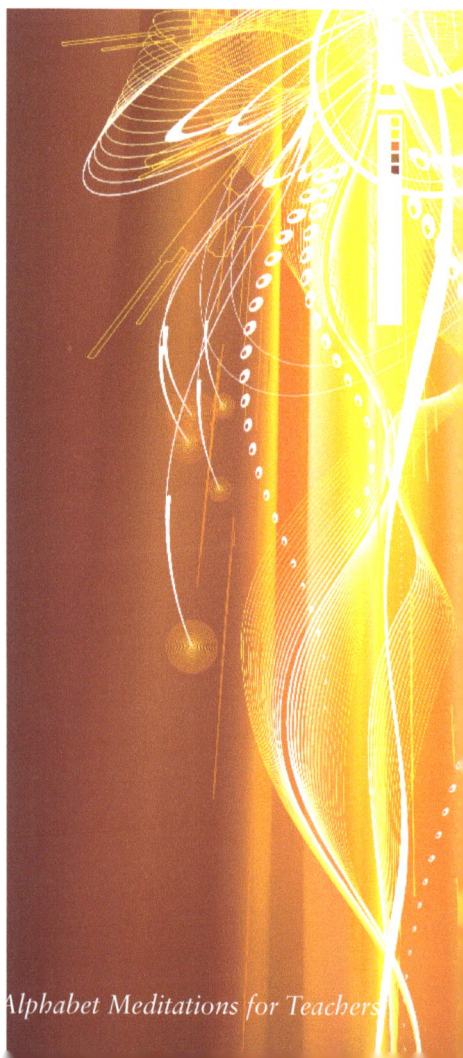

When my—our—canoe
Rides on their flow,
There's power,
Learning, invention.

Help me find the right
Launch. Help me not
Dam the stream.
Help me find the power of their imagination.

## *J* is for Juggler

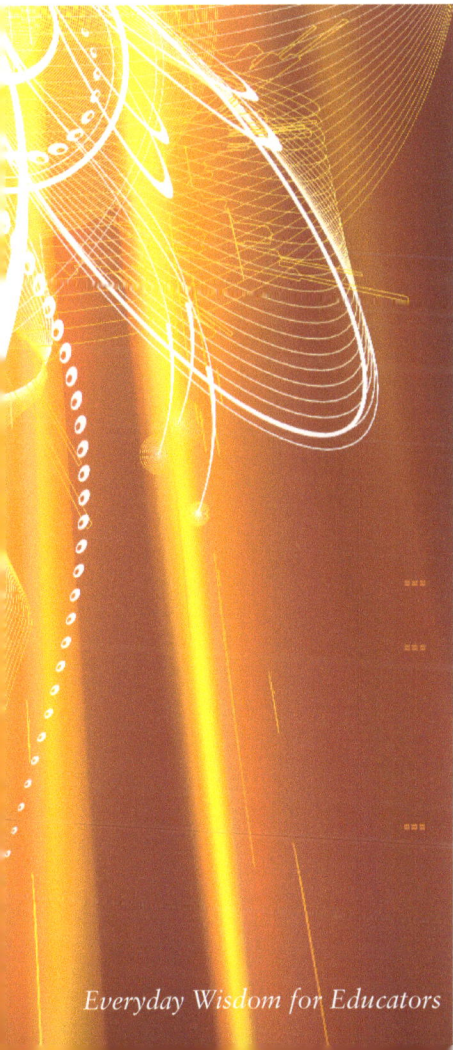

Juggler is my middle name.
I juggle papers,
Books, schedules,
Opened, uneaten crackers.

People's feelings,
Endless meetings,
Then family, friends.
At night, juggle more.

My arms are tired,
Yet they keep moving
Until my life is a
Kaleidoscopic movement—

Blurred images
With no pattern—
Just juggling arms
And endless motion.

Help me stop.
I wasn't born to be
The motor in a
Perpetual machine.
Help me stop.

Drop the balls or pins.
They are not life's substance.
They don't deserve this strain.

When I stop, speak to me.
Tell me to look
At students' faces,
Not the calendar or teacher's guide.

Help me look
Into my own heart,
Not mistake it
For daily announcements.

Lift me from mundane
Into sublime.
Help me know
I work for you.

Teach me to read
Your job description.

## K Is for Kids

Kids. That's why I'm here.
They're not baby goats,
To be sacrificed,
But growing beings.

I hear some say,
"These kids can't. . . ."
"These kids won't. . . ."
"You don't know these kids. . . ."

As if, by herding them
In a group, we can
Label, control, predict
Who/What they are/can be.

When we make
Important decisions,
We say what's good
For teachers, policy,

Bus routes,
Parents' schedules,
Administrative convenience,
Precedent, convention.

Once I heard a small,
Lone voice ask,
"Does anyone care about kids?"
But noise engulfed her.

Help me add my voice
To that one.
Perhaps others will join
To drown out other noise.

Perhaps the day will come
When we ask—in chorus—
On every issue—
"Is this good for kids? Why?"

Oh, Divine Love, help me know
Today, I'm here for them.
To every issue help me ask,
"Is this good for kids?"

Make my voice strong enough
To be heard.

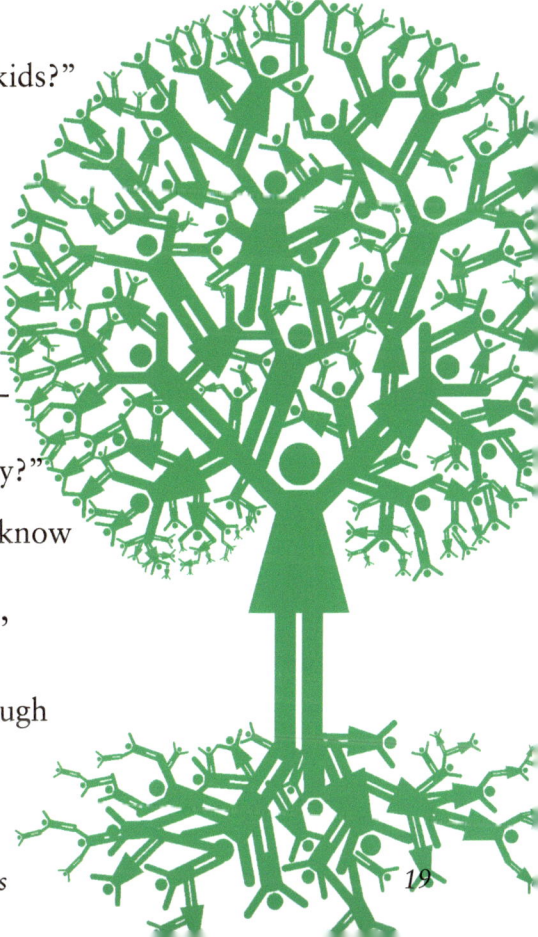

# L Is for Laughter

Laughter is musical—
Healing—release—
Energy—happiness—
Welcome awareness of joy.

Today I vow to
Listen for laughter.
To allow it
In my room.

Help me celebrate
By laughing with it.

Sometimes my laugh
Is so tight—polite—
Forced—unreal—
A front for pleasantry.

Today I release
Real joy within
By letting my own
Laughter out.

I welcome
Humor in my classroom—
Not the raucous,
Hurtful kind,

But the musical,
Lilting, soprano
Laughter that
Comes forth

With beauty
And joy.
That's the laughter
That heals.

*Alphabet Meditations for Teachers*

# M Is for Morning

Morning is awakening—
Soft breezes
Bearing new,
Distant bird calls.

Earth responding to
Love's new-day rays.
Each day, new beginning
For ancient soils.

Today I promise
To feel the hope
Of morning.

It's so hard
To feel rebirth
When my morning
Is laced with hard-edged news,

Traced with black coffee,
Scrunched into a noisy car,
Crammed in traffic,
Packaged with a bow of bells.

It's so hard
To feel renewed
When the familiar
Routes scream "SAME!" to me.

They look mundane—
Gray—I think,
"How long, oh my,
How long?"

And count days
Until vacation—
Or pension.

It's morning.
I know
What it means.
Rebirth. Refresh. Renew.

Today I promise to look at
Faces in my classroom—
See leaves, rocks, birds—
Awaiting signal of first ray.

Make me a good
First ray—
Feel it first in me, then
Radiate it outward.

Today I know
These ancient faces
Before me
Can live again—

Love again—
In a new day.
I know my role.
I promise to live it.
This morning.

## N Is for Names

I remember my name—
And honor who I am.
Help me not use
Names and labels
To control or demean others.

Stop me from calling students
Out of their names by
Thinking of them as
Sluggard, lowly,
Stupid, or lazy.

Make me realize
That, if I think it,
They'll see it
And mirror the behavior
I had hoped to erase.

Sometimes, in my haste,
I trip over the sound of
Their names. The accent
Is wrong—or I'm so
Afraid to get it wrong that I do.

Sometimes, in my prejudice,
I detest their names,
So I stumble over them
Out of fear
And disrespect.

I remember
That these children
Are yours.
Their name is
Holy Child.

I honor
Who they are
And who you are.
I remember and
Love their names.

# O Is for Open

Open doors are
More inviting than closed ones.
I remember a magical
Night at the home of my friend.

As I entered the curved
Drive, lights were ablaze in the house.
The door was wide open;
My loving host was waiting.

Open my eyes to the
Doors I have shut.
Ask for me
Open questions.

Is my face that of
A loving host?
In my room,
Are lights ablaze?

When I speak,
Do I open by
Inviting their ideas,
Or do I close by stating mine?

Stop me from being
The Great Pontificator,
With all the answers
To unasked questions.

Teach me how to
Open their minds
By opening my own.
Help me not fear not knowing.

*Alphabet Meditations for Teachers*

I know my role
Is Great Questioner,
Not Great Answerer,
And Partner in Discovery.

When I'm open,
I find wonder,
Excitement, peace.
So will they.

Hold my hand.
Whisper softly to me,
"Ye shall know the truth,
And the truth shall set you free."

If I'm open.

## P Is for Parents

Teach me that
Parents are doing the best they
Know how to do.
Some of them are
Frightened for survival.
Some are on the streets.

Help me feel,
For just a moment,
Their fear—
To make me
More sensitive to
Its reality.

Some parents are
Terrified of
Losing Social Status.
Help me realize that
The fears that drive them
Are real.

I see that
Their exterior,
Which looks like
Arrogance and Power,
Might mask
Deep fear.

With all parents,
Make me gentle,
My words soft,
So as not to hit them
Where they
Already hurt.

I accept that
My job is not
To fix parents.
My job is
To do my job
Teaching their children.

I am their partner;
We love the same person—
Their child.

Give me grace not to be
Defensive when
They attack,
But to calmly and
Confidently explain
Myself to them.

Make me honest—
True to myself—
True to the
Best knowledge of my profession.

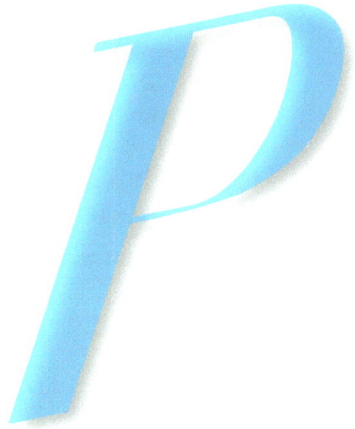

Grant me the faith and
Courage to admit
When I'm wrong,
Apologize, and change.

Help me also have the
Courage to hold my
Head up and speak when
I am right.

Help me know the difference.

Help me not to be afraid—
But to trust Divine Wisdom
To show me
How to love the parents
Of the children I teach.

# Is for Quiet

Quiet is a state of mind—
Even when my
Students can hear a
Pin drop in my room,
Hellish voices,
Intruding from
Other sources,
May be screaming
In their souls.

Maybe that's why
They can't sit still
Or concentrate
Or be polite
Or do their work
I think is so
Almighty important.

I will not add
One more hellish voice
To their cacophony.
No matter what, I will
Be kind. Soft, yet firm.
Setting boundaries,
But gently guiding
These precious ones.

I will not touch
Where it hurts,
To further harm.

Let me—help me—
Soothe.

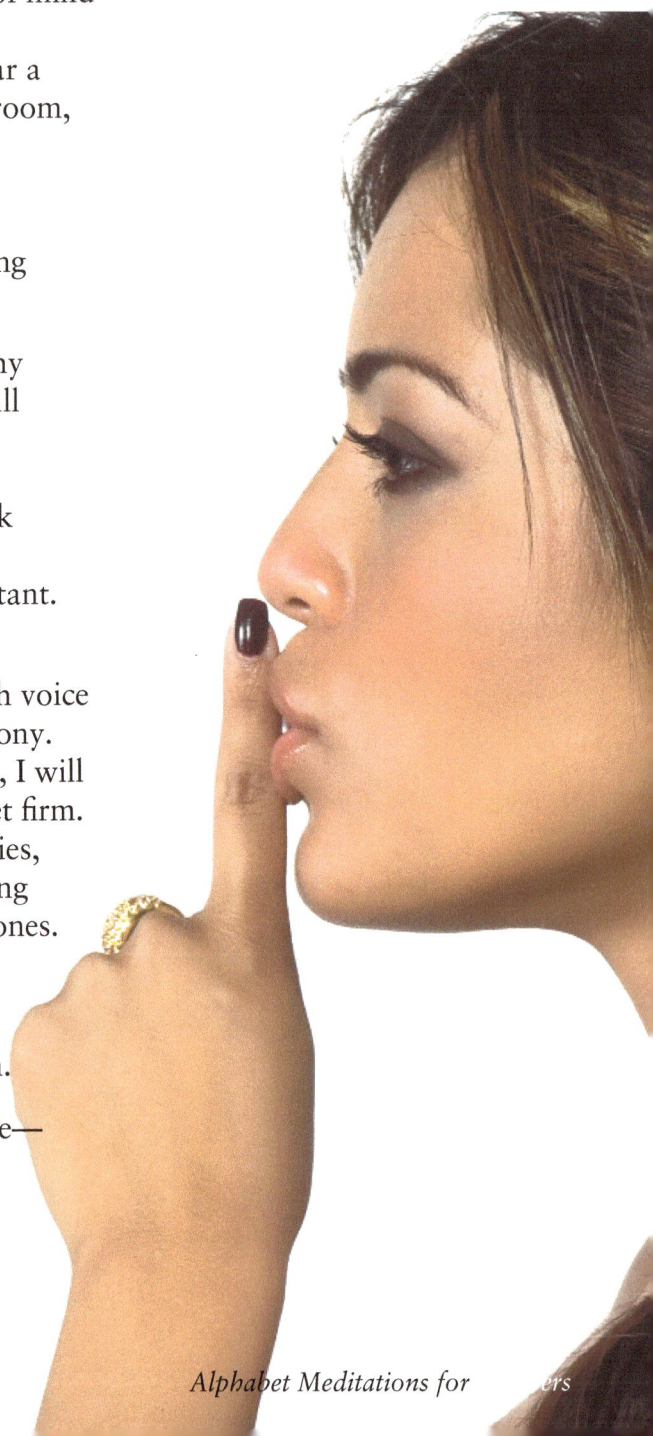

*Alphabet Meditations for* ~~ers~~

# R Is for Rules

Rules govern my
Whole existence.
Those on my wall
Announce to my
Students what will
Happen when they do
This—or that—
And marks beside
Their name keep
The score.

The school handbook has
More rules.
We read them—
Parents sign them
Because we say they
Have to—
Then we—and the
Hallway police—
Enforce them.

I'm so sick of rules.
And hearings to settle
Disputes over who broke
Which rule at what time.
This is not the way
We were meant to live—
With rule books
As our guides.

We were meant to live
In love, following
One rule.

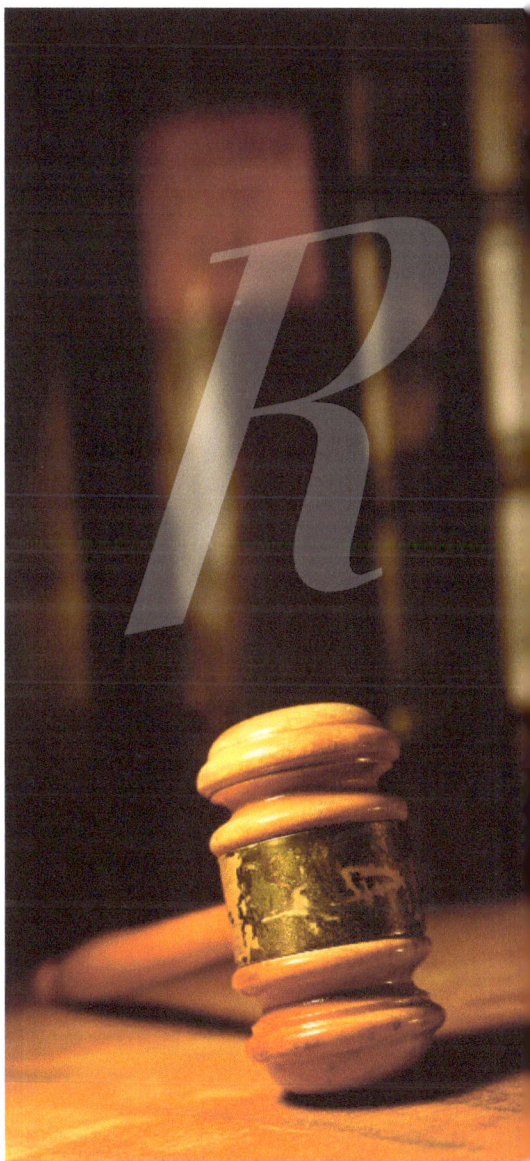

Until we know that
We'll never be able
To hire enough police,
We're lost.

Help me today to
Be a keeper of the
One Best Rule—
To be a healer and friend.

## S Is for Summer

Summer is the time I love.
Long mornings,
Lingering over newspaper,
Book, or mere reverie.

Relaxing on lake or
Mountain—renewing
My spirit—remembering
Who I am.

I promise to bring summer
Into my classroom today.
I promise to have fun
With them while we learn,

As I remember
The refreshment of
Fountains—falls—
Still waters—

Majesty of trees—
Vastness of beach—
Simplicity of campfire—
Beauty of rock.

Today I remember
How open the world is—
And vast—
Today I remember

My classroom
Is not their world.
We are fellows
On this journey.

I am only their guide.
Let me b e a good
Camp Counselor—
A guide deserving trust.

# T Is for Timing

Timing is the key—The
Different key for different locks.

I didn't learn to tie my shoe
Or ride my bike
Or throw the ball
As soon as my friend.

I could never play the piano
As well as Patsy,
And I still can't skip a
Stone across a lake or river.

Not that I can't, you understand.
It's just that I haven't lived long enough
Or wanted to well enough
Or tried in the right way.

Some of my students don't yet
Know basic words or sounds.
They can't read or write
Or think or explain articulately
A concept I've taught for weeks—
Or sing it well or
Do it right.

Help me find the right key
For each lock.

If I'm trying to force my key,
Help me let go—
Be grateful for the
Locks I loosened so easily—

Lovingly embrace
The challenge of finding
New keys for the
Still-solid locks.

Grant me the courage to ask.
Grant me the strength to find.
Help me have the hope
To look into their eyes—
Into my own mind and heart—
And try again.

### U Is for Umbrellas

On rainy days
We bring umbrellas
And place them on the floor
Like wings spread to dry.

Umbrellas.
Bulky bulwarks.
Defense against
The rain.

I saw a woman once
On campus.
The spring rain
Was soft.

She walked slowly,
Without raincoat,
Hat,
Or umbrella.

She savored the rain—
Lifted her
Face to it.
Kissed it.

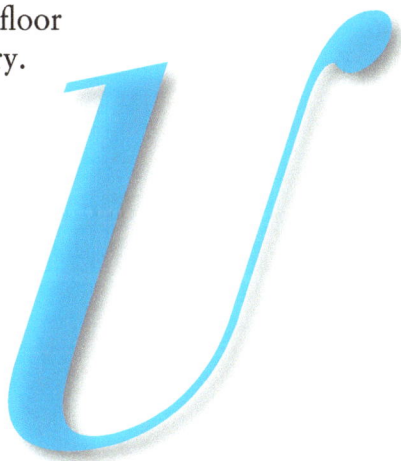

But I bring my
Umbrella.
And they bring
Theirs.

We hunch our
Shoulders beneath them,
Balance our books,
Shut car doors with our heels.

Then splay the
Wired shelter
To trip around
All day.

Why?
Rain isn't
An enemy,
So why defend?

Help me abandon
Unnecessary defenses
That trip me,
Gore my legs,

And get in our way.
Help me know
That some rain
Is required for growth.

Help me speak softly
Of rain—
Embrace it—
Even kiss it.

Umbrellas are man-made;
Rain is your work.
Help me realize
Which one is real.

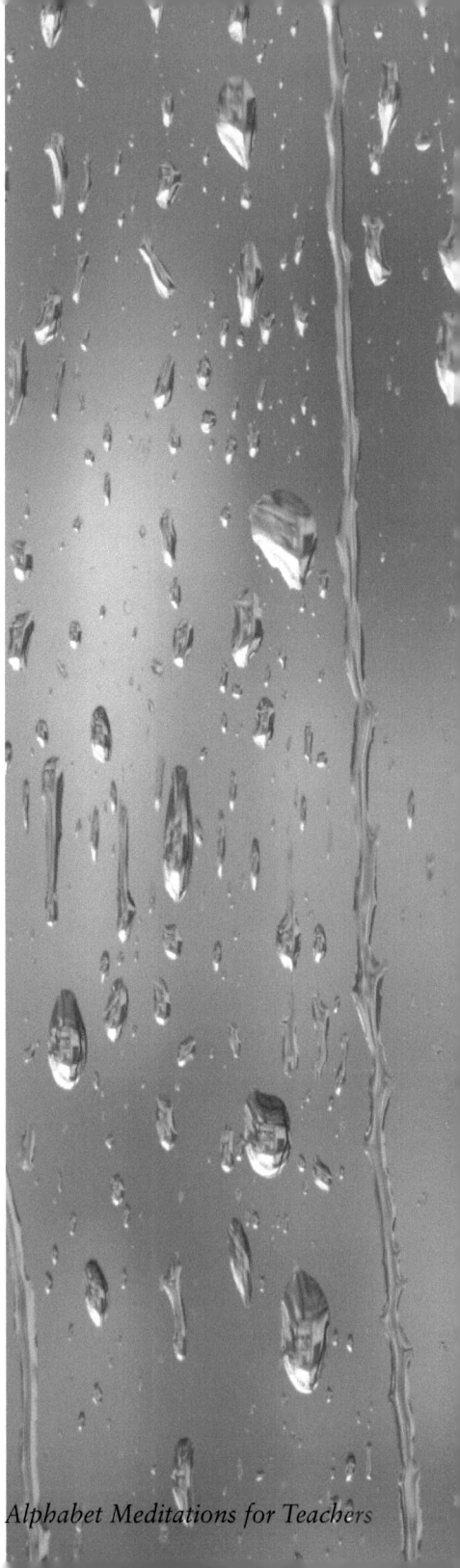

*Alphabet Meditations for Teachers*

## *V* Is for Vacation

I take a vacation
That's really vacation—
To hear what my soul
Wants to say.

Vacation from noise—
Deadlines—
Books—
Papers and grades.

I declare
Vacation tonight
For my soul
To be free.

If only in my mind,
I feel
Cool running streams
On bare feet.

I sense
The freedom
Of first day out of school
Again.

I know that
Vacation is state of mind.
I plan it, take it,
Am renewed by it.

I know that
A refreshed teacher
Is the greatest gift
I can give my students—

More valuable
Than a perfect lesson,
An excellent test,
Or a stack of books.

So tonight
I find
Vacation
In my soul.

## W Is for Window

Help me look out
The window more
To the world of
Wonders outside.

I remember two windows,
Both in spring.
One, on second floor,
Revealed a tree of cedar waxwings.

They jostled the leaves
Alive
As my students
Bowed heads to books.

The other allowed
Lawnmower's annoying
Voice into our reverie
With scent of new-mown grass.

Windows open to
Beauty—distraction—
Grim reality—
Hope.

*Alphabet Meditations for Teachers*

If I have no window
In my classroom,
Help me paint one.
Their world does not end here.

It goes beyond
My walls
And limitations—
Transcends my daily plans.

Help us together
Today to
Remember the windows
Leading beyond.

Help me realize
How vast—
How frightening—
Their world is.

Together with us
Open windows to hope.
If I have no window,
Make one for me.

# X Is for Xanadu

Xanadu is a poem
Written in an opiate dream,
Cryptic and unfinished.

Why did I have to study it
As a student?
Why do I teach it now?

The Venerable Bede—
Who was he?
And why was he venerable?

What does he have to do
With crime in the streets
Or life today?

I choose
What I teach.

I, not the textbook.
Help me choose wisely.
Help me choose well.

Guide me to
Cut the fluff—
To be real.

They trust me
To teach them
What they need to know.

Help me to know
What that is.

Help me listen
When you tell me.

# Y Is for Yesterday

Yesterday is gone.
Vanished.
I can't bring it back
So why does it haunt me so?

The unspoken—
Spoken—words.
The unkind deed.
The job undone.

I bring yesterday
Into today
Too often
And beat myself again.

Worse, I remember
Yesterday's job
From my students,
Full of errors and omissions.

Yet, each day a
New sun breaks.
New breeze blows.
New leaves appear.

Help me allow
Rebirth and fresh starts
Each day.
Help me let go of the past.

Help me forgive the
Slights from others—
The mistakes
They made.

Most of all, help me
Forgive myself.
I'm not perfect—
Don't deserve my own rebuke.

Please take yesterday
And heal it—
Soothe it—
Love it—away.

## Z Is for Zephyr

Zephyr is a warm, playful wind—
No, not wind—
More like air current.

Invisible to the eye,
Felt in the soul,
Warm, friendly, playful.

May zephyr reign today—
In my heart—
In my soul—

Throughout my classroom—
Touching every child—
Every child,

With playful, friendly,
Warm, embrace
Of spirit.

*Alphabet Meditations for Teachers*

# GUIDE FOR USING ALPHABET MEDITA-TIONS AS PROFESSIONAL DEVELOPMENT

*Our brains work best in a state of relaxed alertness.*

Leader says, "Close your eyes. Sit up straight, with your feet flat on the floor and your hands resting lightly on your legs. Take a deep breath—all the way to your navel. Count slowly to 4 on the inhale and 4 on the exhale. Feel the fresh oxygen supply going to your brain and clearing your head. Do this 4 times.

"Now, with your eyes still closed, imagine all those thoughts that have been racing through your mind settling, like sand to the bottom of a glass of water.

[Pause]

"With your eyes still closed, put your hand over your heart. Feel its steady beating as you realize this heart started beating in the third week after your conception, and it is the last organ that will stop functioning when you die. It's with you from beginning to end. It's the truest, purest part of you.

"Listen to your heart. [Pause] What is your heart's desire for today? For someday? What difficulty in your teaching experience needs to be eased right now? What relationship needs to be smoothed?

[Pause]

"Now open your eyes and write these requests on an index card."

**Leader reads one of the meditations, chosen at random. Just open the book to any page and read. Suggest that participants listen with their eyes closed.**

Allow a moment for reflection and then ask, "What became clearer? Write your answer on the index card."

[Pause]

"Now that you are clear, what next step will you take?"

Share what you wrote on the card. What is your heart's desire? What difficulty or relationship needs to be eased or smoothed? What will you do?

While someone is talking, other participants are listening, with no interruption or comment. DO comment if you hear someone saying something you know is not true or correct. Affirm others and yourself.

Say, "As you consistently do this meditation, your intuitive abilities sharpen, and issues take care of themselves, effortlessly. You simply enjoy your relationships with students and parents. Lesson preparation becomes easier and faster. Other professionals interact with you in a cooperative, respectful manner. Your confidence soars as your enjoyment of teaching expands. Things that once seemed difficult now are easy. Go in peace and have a great day!"

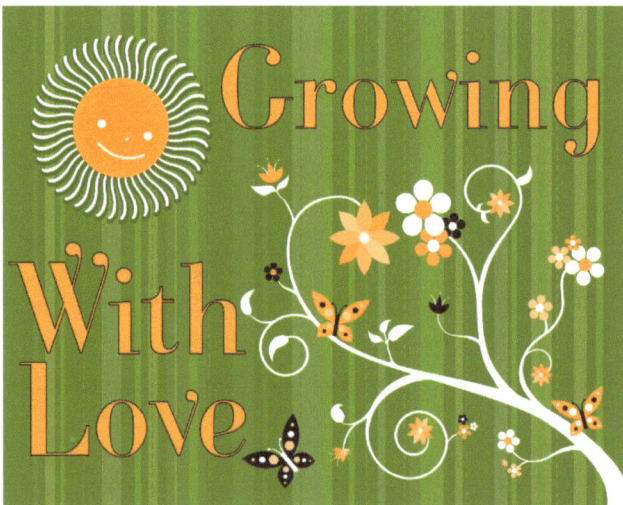

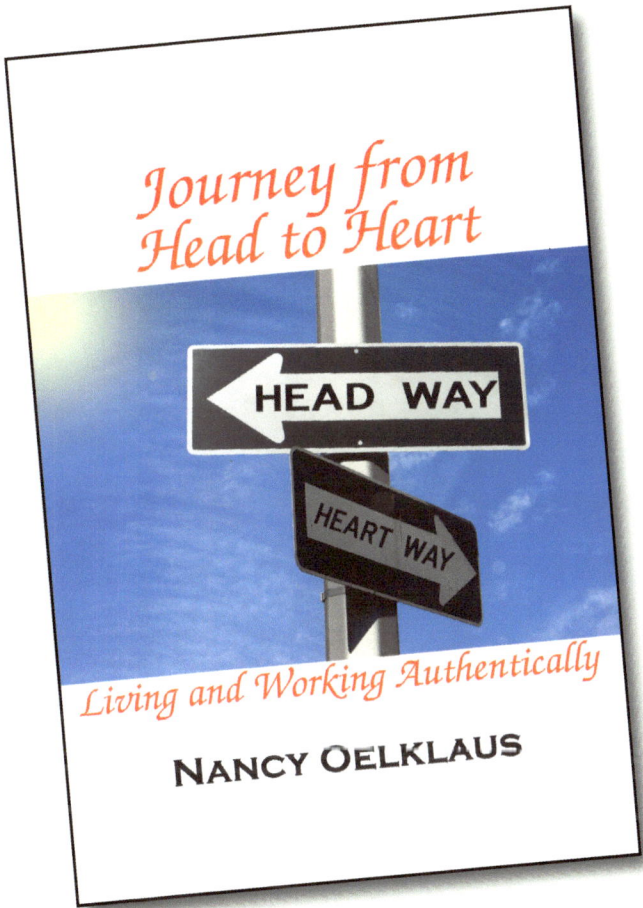

## *Journey From Head to Heart* is...

- **A Toolkit** for those who are exhausted from solving never-ending problems, working harder and harder and not arriving at the destination where they truly want to be.

- **A Map** for how to make the journey from head to heart and then integrate the two so that the power of ego is diminished and the Authentic Self can emerge to live and work from the power of the human spirit.

- **A Reference** book you can use for many years to come as the reader meets life's challenges with success that satisfies both the head and the heart.

# www.HeadtoHeart.com

# Other Great Books for Educators
# from Loving Healing Press

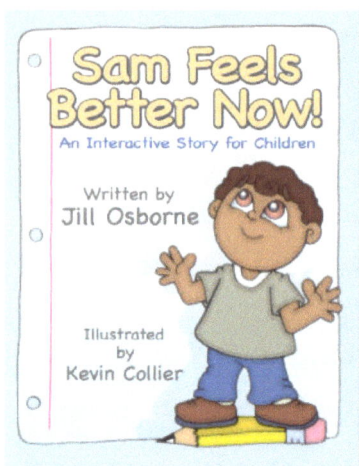

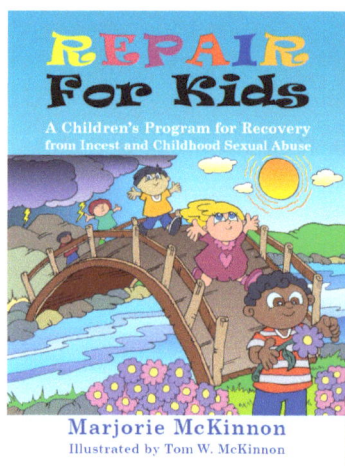

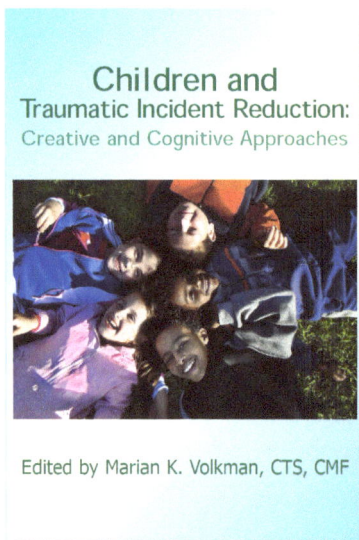

**Sam Feels Better Now!**
An Interactive Story for Children

Written by
Jill Osborne

Illustrated
by
Kevin Collier

**REPAIR For Kids**
A Children's Program for Recovery from Incest and Childhood Sexual Abuse

Marjorie McKinnon
Illustrated by Tom W. McKinnon

**Children and Traumatic Incident Reduction:**
Creative and Cognitive Approaches

Edited by Marian K. Volkman, CTS, CMF

**THE WHOLE YOUTH WORKER**
Advice on Professional, Personal, and Physical Wellness from the Trenches
JAY TUCKER

www.LovingHealing.com

# Billy Had To Move

Theresa Ann Fraser, CYW, B.A.
Illustrated by Alex Walton

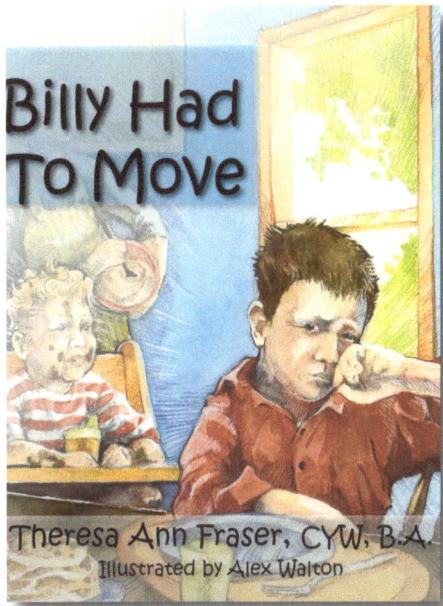

> "...a much-needed book for foster care children to help them in adjusting to a new caregiver and placement."
>
> Athena A. Drewes, PsyD
> Director of Clinical Training
> Astor Home for Children,
> Poughkeepsie, NY

Child Protection Services have been involved with Billy and his mother for some time now. He has been happily settled in a kinship placement with his grandmother and enjoys his pet cat, interacting with neighbors and even taking piano lessons. As the story unfolds, Billy's grandmother has unexpectedly passed away and so the story of *Billy Had To Move* begins.

Unfortunately, Billy's mother cannot be located. Mr. Murphy, Billy's social worker, places him in the foster home of Amy, Tim, and their baby "Colly." Billy experiences great loss resulting not only from his grandmother's death, but also the loss of the life he knew. Billy's inner journey therefore has also begun and with the help of Ms. Woods, a Play Therapist, there is hope.

www.TheresaFraser.com

www.ingramcontent.com/pod-product-compliance
Lightning Source LLC
Chambersburg PA
CBHW042107110426
42742CB00033BA/23